This book belongs to

_____

This book is dedicated to my children – Mikey, Kobe, and Jojo.
Gratitude heals your mind, body, and spirit.

Grateful Ninja

By Mary Nhin

Pictures by
Jelena Stupar

If you ever ran into Grateful Ninja, she was probably thanking someone or something.

But Grateful Ninja was not always like this.

Once upon a time, she really could be quite ungrateful and unhappy.

When she received a gift, she would forget to say thank you!

And if she was asking for something, it wasn't important to her to say please.

When she played outside, she never took notice of the marvel of the world around her.

Yes, Grateful Ninja was not very grateful or happy. But that changed one day when she and Calm Ninja made a pact to be more appreciative.

It didn't take long for the two to come up with some really great ideas. And they soon put it into motion:

1. Grow our thank-yous and pleases.

2. Gift ourselves a gratitude jar.

Everyday, we'll add a note of what we're grateful for in the jar.

Give gratitude at the dinner table and before bedtime.

4.

Get a gratitude journal.

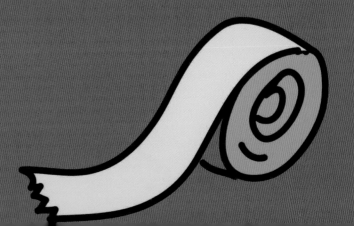

Can you guess how Grateful Ninja felt after the five days?

If you guessed happy or grateful, you are correct.

Grateful Ninja couldn't remember when she felt happier. To her surprise, it didn't take a gift, new toy, or game to get her there.

She began to appreciate the simple things, both big and small.

The 5 Gs

1. Grow our thank-yous and pleases.
2. Gift ourselves a gratitude jar.
3. Give gratitude at the dinner table and before bedtime.
4. Get a gratitude journal.
5. Go on a gratitude nature walk.

Remembering the 5 Gs could be your secret weapon against unhappiness.

Check out Grateful Ninja's Gratitude Journal on Amazon to build your gratitude! And please leave a kind review, we would be so GRATEFUL!

 @marynhin   @GrowGrit
#NinjaLifeHacks

 Mary Nhin   Grow Grit

▶ Grow Grit